Wm. F. Curtis.

June '08.

Riverside Educational Monographs

EDITED BY HENRY SUZZALLO

PROFESSOR OF THE PHILOSOPHY OF EDUCATION
TEACHERS COLLEGE, COLUMBIA UNIVERSITY

SELF-CULTIVATION
IN ENGLISH

BY

GEORGE HERBERT PALMER

ALFORD PROFESSOR OF PHILOSOPHY
HARVARD UNIVERSITY

HOUGHTON MIFFLIN COMPANY

BOSTON, NEW YORK AND CHICAGO

The Riverside Press, Cambridge

INTRODUCTION

ENGLISH as a school subject grows more important in the education of our youth. Its place in our schools begins to be as large as its position in every-day life. And gradually the aims pursued by the school in English teaching conform to those practical and artistic purposes which are usually associated with our spoken and written language.

Educational reform and English study

The teaching of English reflects the important movements for the reform of our schools. There is, indeed, no better index of our substantial achievements in modern educational affairs than those modifications in English instruction which are now in progress. The passing of a technical and barren study of grammatical and rhetorical forms is part of the general tendency toward the subordination of formal subjects. The introduction of classic material in reading books and the study of unmarred literary wholes mark the determined effort to enrich the school curriculum with content significant alike to the child and to the society in which he lives. The increased emphasis on English composition as an instrument for the communication or expression of the child's thought is a response to the same ideals of educational method which are giving manual training and the other expressive arts a respectable position in the school curriculum.

Changes in the spirit of English instruction

The influence of educational reform on English instruction extends beyond specific changes in the subject matter and methods used in schools. It causes wide-sweeping modifications in the whole spirit of our English teaching. Slowly but certainly it dawns on us that a mere study of the formalities of language does not insure an enjoyment of literature or a command of speech. In place of the old and barren insistence upon a half-scientific analysis of language which leaves us conscious only of the dissected parts

INTRODUCTION

of language, modern teaching sets up two new major purposes for English study, — to develop an appreciation of the best English literature, and to train the power of effective expression through language.

The difficulty of training linguistic power

It is the attainment of this latter end, the improved use of English as an instrument of expression, that presents the largest difficulties to the teacher. Most of the current practices of the school have been developed mainly with reference to giving the child the facts of our organized knowledge. Until recently, its methods have not been concerned with training him in the application or expression of the thoughts thus attained. Hence the weakness of the school in teaching children to speak and write good English is conspicuous, and hence the need to improve the conditions that underlie the acquirement of clear and forceful expression and to develop new modes of transmitting the technique of English speech and writing.

INTRODUCTION

Conditions have been unfavorable

The schools of to-day find it difficult to undertake the training of literary power because unfavorable conditions persist from the schools of a century ago. Time was when any deliberate effort to teach children to write in school would have largely failed because there was no clear recognition of the fact that there can be no cultivation of the power to use English without an adequate development of enriched thought to be expressed. That older school which was mainly concerned with the formal subjects — the three R's, grammar, rhetoric, and the like — gave children little that could be the basis of real, written composition. True expression is always self-expression, and for self-expression more is required than the committing to memory of ideas. The schools of that other day, in so far as they contributed to the knowledge of children, imposed it upon them authoritatively, without any special consideration of their interests or needs. What the school asked children to express, they had no desire to express ; and what they might choose to say, the school regarded as trivial. Hence our poverty of literary power in the schools has descended to us along with dull courses of study and dogmatic methods of teaching.

Conditions grow more favorable

The newer movements in education tend to establish conditions which are a striking contrast to those of the past. The course of study has been enriched by the addition of new subjects and by the vitalization of old studies. First-hand contact with the natural world and with human life is guaranteed as never before. Much of the acquisition of knowledge is closely connected with active ways of learning. Above all, there is a sympathy for children which recognizes that true education must start with the vital impulses of child-life. Under such an order children have something to say, and they want to say it. And teachers are willing to listen or read, as the case may be, knowing that the forces which make for literary power are there, ready to be restrained or refined as the canons of good taste and clear expression demand.

INTRODUCTION

Methods of improving literary power

Now that we have our children speaking and writing we need to know how we can improve those crude talents which instinct and a favorable school life permit. The problem is a new one for the pedagogue, for the transmission of the power to write is very different from the transmission of grammatical or rhetorical facts. Indeed, it may be said that we cannot transmit the power of using English. In the last analysis, good English usage is a matter of self-cultivation. The teacher, however, can supervise the process of self-development. By insuring a rich thought-life, by fostering opportunities for its expression, by encouraging worthy effort, by providing practice for right speech, and by attending to the hundred other details which are a necessary care, the teacher may help the present generation to achieve the ability to use with force and grace their mother tongue that has come to its present power and beauty only after many generations of refined development. But there can be no effective self-cultivation in English, or helpful direction of the same, without some knowledge of the technical processes by which literary power is to be attained. There must be some knowledge of the way the deed is done, some hint of the factors that make for good expression.

A guide for students and teacher

With the above need in mind, there is here presented an essay on " Self-Cultivation in English." At once a clear analysis of the fundamental elements in the noble use of language and a fine example of the use of good English, it is offered to the public with a sense of its double worth. While it is strongly commended to students in our higher schools as a guide and model for them in their effort to improve their use of English, it is primarily included within this series in order that teachers and parents may have its assistance in focusing their attention upon those matters of large importance in speaking and writing which must be the care of all who would make of their own expression a worthy model and guide for others.

SELF-CULTIVATION IN ENGLISH

SELF-CULTIVATION IN ENGLISH

ENGLISH study has four aims: the mastery of our language as a science, as a history, as a joy, and as a tool. I am concerned with but one, the mastery of it as a tool. Philology and grammar present it as a science; the one attempting to follow its words, the other its sentences, through all the intricacies of their growth, and so to manifest laws which lie hidden in these airy products no less than in the moving stars or the myriad flowers of spring. Fascinating and important as all this is, I do not recommend it here. For I want to call attention only to that sort of English study which can be carried on without any large apparatus of books. For a reason similar, though less cogent, I do not urge historical study. Probably the current of English literature is more attractive through its continuity than that of any other nation. Notable works in verse and prose have appeared in long succession,

I

and without gaps intervening, in a way that
would be hard to parallel in any other language
known to man. A bounteous endowment this
for every English speaker, and one which should
stimulate us to trace the marvelous and close-
linked progress from the times of the Saxons to
those of Tennyson and Kipling. Literature, too,
has this advantage over every other species of
art study, that everybody can examine the origi-
nal masterpieces and not depend on reproduc-
tions, as in the cases of painting, sculpture, and
architecture ; or on intermediate interpretation,
as in the case of music. To-day most of these
masterpieces can be bought for a trifle, and even
a poor man can follow through centuries the
thoughts of his ancestors. But even so, ready of
access as it is, English can be studied as a history only at the cost of solid time and continuous
attention, much more time than the majority of
those I am addressing can afford. By most of us
our mighty literature cannot be taken in its continuous current, the later stretches proving interesting through relation with the earlier. It must
be taken fragmentarily, if at all, the attention

delaying on those parts only which offer the greatest beauty or promise the best exhilaration. In other words, English may be possible as a joy where it is not possible as a history. In the endless wealth which our poetry, story, essay, and drama afford, every disposition may find its appropriate nutriment, correction, or solace. He is unwise, however busy, who does not have his loved authors, veritable friends with whom he takes refuge in the intervals of work, and by whose intimacy he enlarges, refines, sweetens, and emboldens his own limited existence. Yet the fact that English as a joy must largely be conditioned by individual taste prevents me from offering general rules for its pursuits. The road which leads one man straight to enjoyment leads another to tedium. In all literary enjoyment there is something incalculable, something wayward, eluding the precision of rule and rendering inexact the precepts of him who would point out the path to it. While I believe that many suggestions may be made, useful to the young enjoyer, and promotive of his wise vagrancy, I shall not undertake here the complicated task of

3

offering them. Let enjoyment go, let history go, let science go, and still English remains — English as a tool. Every hour our language is an engine for communicating with others, every instant for fashioning the thoughts of our own minds. I want to call attention to the means of mastering this curious and essential tool, and to lead every one who hears me to become discontented with his employment of it.

The importance of literary power needs no long argument. Everybody acknowledges it, and sees that without it all other human faculties are maimed. Shakespeare says that "Time insults o'er dull and speechless tribes." It and all who live in it insult over the speechless person. So mutually dependent are we that on our swift and full communication with one another is staked the success of almost every scheme we form. He who can explain himself may command what he wants. He who cannot is left to the poverty of individual resource; for men do what we desire only when persuaded. The persuasive and explanatory tongue is, therefore, one of the chief levers of life. Its leverage is felt within us as well as without, for expression and thought are integrally bound together. We do not first possess completed thoughts, and then express them. The very formation of the outward product extends, sharpens, enriches the mind which produces, so that he who gives forth little, after a time is likely enough to discover that he has little to give forth. By expression, too, we may carry our benefits and our names to a far generation. This durable character of fragile language puts a wide difference of worth between it and some of the other great objects of desire, — health, wealth, and beauty, for example. These are notoriously liable to accident. We tremble while we have them. But literary power, once ours, is more likely than any other possession to be ours always. It perpetuates and enlarges itself by the very fact of its existence, and perishes only with the decay of the man himself. For this reason, because more than health, wealth, and beauty, literary style may be called the man, good judges have found in it the final test of culture, and have said that he and he alone, is a well-educated person who uses his language with power and beauty. The supreme and ultimate product of civilization, it has been well said, is two or three persons talking together in a room. Between ourselves and our language there accordingly springs up an association peculiarly close. We are as sensitive to criticism of our speech as of our manners. The young man looks up with awe to him who has written a book, as already half divine ; and the graceful speaker is a universal object of envy.

But the very fact that literary endowment is immediately recognized and eagerly envied has induced a strange illusion in regard to it. It is supposed to be something mysterious, innate in him who possesses it, and quite out of the reach of him who has it not. The very contrary is the fact. No human employment is more free and calculable than the winning of language. Undoubtedly there are natural aptitudes for it, as there are for farming, seamanship, or being a good husband. But nowhere is straight work more effective. Persistence, care, discriminating observation, ingenuity, refusal to lose heart, — traits which in every other occupation tend toward excellence, — tend

6

toward it here with special security. Whoever goes to his grave with bad English in his mouth has no one to blame but himself for the disagreeable taste; for if faulty speech can be inherited, it can be exterminated too. I hope to point out some of the methods of substituting good English for bad. And since my space is brief, and I wish to be remembered, I throw what I have to say into the form of four simple precepts, which, if pertinaciously obeyed, will, I believe, give anybody effective mastery of English as a tool.

First, then, "Look well to your speech." It is commonly supposed that when a man seeks literary power he goes to his room and plans an article for the press. But this is to begin literary culture at the wrong end. We speak a hundred times for every once we write. The busiest writer produces little more than a volume a year, not so much as his talk would amount to in a week. Consequently through speech it is usually decided whether a man is to have command of his language or not. If he is slovenly in his ninety-nine cases of talking, he can seldom pull himself up to strength and exactitude in the hundredth case of writing. A person is made in one piece, and the same being runs through a multitude of performances. Whether words are uttered on paper or to the air, the effect on the utterer is the same. Vigor or feebleness results according as energy or slackness has been in command. I know that certain adaptations to a new field are often necessary. A good speaker may find awkwardness in himself when he comes to write, a good writer when he speaks. And certainly cases occur where a man exhibits distinct strength in one of the two, speaking or writing, and not in the other. But such cases are rare. As a rule, language once within our control can be employed for oral or for written purposes. And since the opportunities for oral practice enormously outbalance those for written, it is the oral which are chiefly significant in the development of literary power. We rightly say of the accomplished writer that he shows a mastery of his own tongue.

This predominant influence of speech marks nearly all great epochs of literature. The Homeric poems are addressed to the ear, not to the eye. It is doubtful if Homer knew writing, certain that he knew profoundly every quality of the tongue, — veracity, vividness, shortness of sentence, simplicity of thought, obligation to insure swift apprehension. Writing and rigidity are apt to go together. In these smooth-slipping verses one catches everywhere the voice. So, too, the aphorisms of Hesiod might naturally pass from mouth to mouth, and the stories of Herodotus be told by an old man at the fireside. Early Greek literature is plastic and garrulous. Its distinctive glory is that it contains no literary note; that it gives forth human feeling not in conventional arrangement, but with apparent spontaneity — in short, that it is speech literature, not book literature. And the same tendency continued long among the Greeks. At the culmination of their power, the drama was their chief literary form, — the drama, which is but speech ennobled, connected, clarified. Plato too, following the dramatic precedent and the precedent of his talking master, accepted conversation as his medium for philosophy, and imparted to it the vivacity, ease, waywardness even, which the best conversation exhibits. Nor was the experience of the Greeks peculiar. Our literature shows a similar tendency. Its bookish times are its decadent times, its talking times its glory. Chaucer, like Herodotus, is a story-teller, and follows the lead of those who on the Continent entertained courtly circles with pleasant tales. Shakespeare and his fellows in the spacious times of great Elizabeth did not concern themselves with publication. Marston, in one of his prefaces, thinks it necessary to apologize for putting his piece in print, and says he would not have done such a thing if unscrupulous persons, hearing the play at the theatre, had not already printed corrupt versions of it. Even the "Queen Anne's men," far removed though they are from anything dramatic, still shape their ideals of literature by demands of speech. The essays of the "Spectator," the poems of Pope, are the remarks of a cultivated gentleman at an evening party. Here is the brevity, the good taste, the light touch, the neat epigram, the avoidance of whatever might stir passion, controversy, or laborious thought, which characterize the conversation of a well-bred man. Indeed, it is hard to see how any literature can be long vital which is based on the thought of a book and not on that of living utterance. Unless the speech notion is uppermost, words will not run swiftly to their mark. They delay in delicate phrasings while naturalness and a sense of reality disappear. Women are the best talkers. I sometimes please myself with noticing that three of the greatest periods of English literature coincide with the reigns of the three English queens.

Fortunate it is, then, that self-cultivation in the use of English must chiefly come through speech; because we are always speaking, whatever else we do. In opportunities for acquiring a mastery of language, the poorest and busiest are at no large disadvantage as compared with the leisured rich. It is true the strong impulse which comes from the suggestion and approval of society may in some cases be absent, but this can be compensated by the sturdy purpose of the learner. A recognition of the beauty of well-ordered words, a strong desire, patience under discouragements, and promptness in counting every occasion as of consequence, — these are the simple agencies which sweep one on to power. Watch your speech, then. That is all which is needed. Only it is desirable to know what qualities of speech to watch for. I find three, — accuracy, audacity, and range, — and I will say a few words about each.

Obviously, good English is exact English. Our words should fit our thoughts like a glove, and be neither too wide nor too tight. If too wide, they will include much vacuity beside the intended matter. If too tight, they will check the strong grasp. Of the two dangers, looseness is by far the greater. There are people who say what they mean with such a naked precision that nobody not familiar with the subject can quickly catch the sense. George Herbert and Emerson strain the attention of many. But niggardly and angular speakers are rare. Too frequently words signify nothing in particular. They are merely thrown out in a certain direction, to report a vague and undetermined meaning or even a general emotion. The first business of every one who would train himself in language is to articulate his thought, to know definitely what he wishes to say, and then to pick those words which compel the hearer to think of this and only this. For such a purpose two words are often better than three. The fewer the words, the more pungent the impression. Brevity is the soul not simply of a jest, but of wit in its finest sense where it is identical with wisdom. He who can put a great deal into a little is the master. Since firm texture is what is wanted, not embroidery or superposed ornament, beauty has been well defined as the purgation of superfluities. And certainly many a paragraph might have its beauty brightened by letting quiet words take the place of its loud words, omitting its "verys," and striking out its purple patches of "fine writing." Here is Ben Jonson's description of Bacon's language : "There happened in my time one noble speaker who was full of gravity in his speech. No man ever spoke more neatly, more pressly, more weightily, or suffered less emptiness, less idleness, in what he uttered. No member of his speech but consisted of his own graces. His hearers could not cough or look aside without loss. He commanded when he spoke, and had his judges angry or pleased at his discretion." Such are the men who command, men who speak "neatly and pressly." But to gain such precision is toilsome business. While we are in training for it, no word must unpermittedly pass the portal of the teeth. Something like what we mean must never be counted equivalent to what we mean. And if we are not sure of our meaning or of our word, we must pause until we are sure. Accuracy does not come of itself. For persons who can use several languages, capital practice in acquiring it can be had by translating from one language to another and seeing that the entire sense is carried over. Those who have only their native speech will find it profitable often to attempt definitions of the common words they use. Inaccuracy will not stand up against the habit of definition. Dante boasted that no rhythmic exigency had ever made him say what he did not mean. We heedless and unintending speakers, under no exigency of rhyme or reason, say what we mean but seldom, and still more seldom mean what we

say. To hold our thoughts and words in significant adjustment requires unceasing consciousness, a perpetual determination not to tell lies;
for of course every inaccuracy is a bit of un-
truthfulness. We have something in mind, yet
convey something else to our hearer. And no
moral purpose will save us from this untruthful-
ness unless that purpose is sufficient to inspire
the daily drill which brings the power to be true.
Again and again we are shut up to evil because
we have not acquired the ability of goodness.

But after all, I hope that nobody who hears
me will quite agree. There is something enervat-
ing in conscious care. Necessary as it is in
shaping our purposes, if allowed too direct and
exclusive control consciousness breeds hesitation
and feebleness. Action is not excellent, at least,
until spontaneous. In piano-playing we begin by
picking out each separate note; but we do not
call the result music until we play our notes by
the handful, heedless how each is formed. And so
it is everywhere. Consciously selective conduct
is elementary and inferior. People distrust it, or
rather they distrust him who exhibits it. If any-

body talking to us visibly studies his words, we turn away. What he says may be well enough as school exercise, but it is not conversation. Accordingly if we would have our speech forcible, we shall need to put into it quite as much of audacity as we do of precision, terseness, or simplicity. Accuracy alone is not a thing to be sought, but accuracy and dash. It was said of Fox, the English orator and statesman, that he was accustomed to throw himself headlong into the middle of a sentence, trusting to God Almighty to get him out. So must we speak. We must not, before beginning a sentence, decide what the end shall be; for if we do, nobody will care to hear that end. At the beginning, it is the beginning which claims the attention of both speaker and listener and trepidation about going on will mar all. We must give our thought its head, and not drive it with too tight a rein, or grow timid when it begins to prance a bit. Of course we must retain coolness in courage, applying the results of our previous discipline in accuracy; but we need not move so slowly as to become formal. Pedantry is worse than blundering. If we care for grace and flexible beauty of language, we must learn to let our thought run. Would it, then, be too much of an Irish bull to say that in acquiring English we need to cultivate spontaneity? The uncultivated kind is not worth much; it is wild and haphazard stuff, unadjusted to its uses. On the other hand, no speech is of much account, however just, which lacks the element of courage. Accuracy and dash, then, the combination of the two, must be our difficult aim; and we must not rest satisfied so long as either dwells with us alone.

But are the two so hostile as they at first appear? Or can, indeed, the first be obtained without the aid of the second? Supposing we are convinced that words possess no value in themselves, and are correct or incorrect only as they truly report experience, we shall feel ourselves impelled in the mere interest of accuracy to choose them freshly, and to put them together in ways in which they never coöperated before, so as to set forth with distinctness that which just we, not other people, have seen or felt. The reason why we do not naturally have this daring exactitude is probably twofold. We let our experiences be blurred, not observing sharply, or knowing with any minuteness what we are thinking about ; and so there is no individuality in our language. And then, besides, we are terrorized by custom, and inclined to adjust what we would say to what others have said before. The cure for the first of these troubles is to keep our eye on our object, instead of on our listener or ourselves ; and for the second, to learn to rate the expressiveness of language more highly than its correctness. The opposite of this, the disposition to set correctness above expressiveness, produces that peculiarly vulgar diction known as "school-ma'am English," in which for the sake of a dull accord with usage all the picturesque, imaginative, and forceful employment of words is sacrificed. Of course we must use words so that people can understand them, and understand them, too, with ease; but this once granted, let our language be our own, obedient to our special needs. "Whenever," says Thomas Jefferson, "by small grammatical negligences the energy of an idea can be condensed or a word be made to stand for a sentence, I hold grammatical rigor in contempt." "Young man," said Henry Ward Beecher to one who was pointing out grammatical errors in a sermon of his, "when the English language gets in my way, it doesn't stand a chance." No man can be convincing, writer or speaker, who is afraid to send his words wherever they may best follow his meaning, and this with but little regard to whether any other person's words have ever been there before. In assessing merit, let us not stupefy ourselves with using negative standards. What stamps a man as great is not freedom from faults, but abundance of powers.

Such audacious accuracy, however, distinguishing as it does noble speech from commonplace speech, can be practised only by him who has a wide range of words. Our ordinary range is absurdly narrow. It is important, therefore, for anybody who would cultivate himself in English to make strenuous and systematic efforts to enlarge his vocabulary. Our dictionaries contain more than a hundred thousand words. The average speaker employs about three thousand. Is this because ordinary people have only three or four thousand things to say? Not at all. It is simply due to dullness. Listen to the average school-boy. He has a dozen or two nouns, half a dozen verbs, three or four adjectives, and enough conjunctions and prepositions to stick the conglomerate together. This ordinary speech deserves the description which Hobbes gave to his " State of Nature," that "it is solitary, poor, nasty, brutish, and short." The fact is, we fall into the way of thinking that the wealthy words are for others, and that they do not belong to us. We are like those who have received a vast inheritance, but who persist in the inconveniences of hard beds, scanty food, rude clothing, who never travel, and who limit their purchases to the bleak necessities of life. Ask such people why they endure niggardly living while wealth in plenty is lying in the bank, and they can only answer that they have never learned how to spend. But this is worth learning. Milton used eight thousand words, Shakespeare fifteen thousand. We have all the subjects to talk about that these early speakers had; and in addition, we have bicycles and sciences and strikes and political combinations and all the complicated living of the modern world.

Why, then, do we hesitate to swell our words to meet our needs? It is a nonsense question. There is no reason. We are simply lazy; too lazy to make ourselves comfortable. We let our vocabularies be limited, and get along rawly without the refinements of human intercourse, without refinements in our own thoughts; for thoughts are almost as dependent on words as words on thoughts. For example, all exasperations we lump together as "aggravating," not considering whether they may not rather be displeasing, annoying, offensive, disgusting, irritating, or even maddening; and without observing, too, that in our reckless usage we have burned up a word which might be convenient when we should need to mark some shading of the word "increase." Like the bad cook, we seize the frying-pan whenever we need to fry, broil, roast, or stew, and then we wonder why all our dishes taste alike while in the next house the food is appetizing. It is all unnecessary.

SELF-CULTIVATION

Enlarge the vocabulary. Let any one who wants to see himself grow, resolve to adopt two new words each week. It will not be long before the endless and enchanting variety of the world will begin to reflect itself in his speech, and in his mind as well. I know that when we use a word for the first time we are startled, as if a firecracker went off in our neighborhood. We look about hastily to see if any one has noticed. But finding that no one has, we may be emboldened. A word used three times slips off the tongue with entire naturalness. Then it is ours forever, and with it some phase of life which had been lacking hitherto. For each word presents its own point of view, discloses a special aspect of things, reports some little importance not otherwise conveyed, and so contributes its small emancipation to our tied-up minds and tongues.

But a brief warning may be necessary to make my meaning clear. In urging the addition of new words to our present poverty-stricken stock, I am far from suggesting that we should seek out strange, technical, or inflated expressions, which do not appear in ordinary conversation. The very opposite is my aim. I would put every man who is now employing a diction merely local and personal in command of the approved resources of the English language. Our poverty usually comes through provinciality, through accepting without criticism the habits of our special set. My family, my immediate friends, have a diction of their own. Plenty of other words, recognized as sound, are known to be current in books, and to be employed by modest and intelligent speakers, only we do not use them. Our set has never said "diction," or "current," or " scope," or "scanty," or "hitherto," or "convey," or "lack." Far from unusual as these words are, to adopt them might seem to set me apart from those whose intellectual habits I share. From this I shrink. I do not like to wear clothes suitable enough for others, but not in the style of my own plain circle. Yet if each one of that circle does the same, the general shabbiness is increased. The talk of all is made narrow enough to fit the thinnest there. What we should seek is to contribute to each of the little companies with which our life is bound up a gently enlarging influence, such impulses as will not startle or create detachment, but which may save from humdrum, routine, and dreary usualness. We cannot be really kind without being a little venturesome. The small shocks of our increasing vocabulary will in all probability be as helpful to our friends as to ourselves.

Such, then, are the excellences of speech. If we would cultivate ourselves in the use of English, we must make our daily talk accurate, daring, and full. I have insisted on these points the more because in my judgment all literary power, especially that of busy men, is rooted in sound speech. But though the roots are here, the growth is also elsewhere. And I pass to my later precepts, which, if the earlier one has been laid well to heart, will require only brief discussion.

Secondly, "Welcome every opportunity for writing." Important as I have shown speech to be, there is much that it cannot do. Seldom can it teach structure. Its space is too small. Talking moves in sentences, and rarely demands a paragraph. I make my little remark, — a dozen or two words, — then wait for my friend to hand me back as many more. This gentle exchange continues by the hour; but either of us would feel himself unmannerly if he should grasp an entire five minutes and make it uninterruptedly his. That would not be speaking, but rather speech-making. The brief groupings of words which make up our talk furnish capital practice in precision, boldness, and variety; but they do not contain room enough for exercising our constructive faculties. Considerable length is necessary if we are to learn how to set forth B in right relation to A on the one hand, and to C on the other; and while keeping each a distinct part, are to be able through their smooth progression to weld all the parts together into a compacted whole. Such wholeness is what we mean by literary form. Lacking it, any piece of writing is a failure; because, in truth, it is not a piece, but pieces. For ease of reading, or for the attainment of an intended effect, unity is essential — the multitude of statements, anecdotes, quotations, arguings, gay sportings, and appeals, all "bending one way their gracious influence." And this dominant unity of the entire piece obliges unity also in the subordinate parts. Not enough has been done when we have huddled together a lot of wandering sentences, and penned them in a paragraph, or even when we have linked them together by the frail ties of "and, and." A sentence must be compelled to say a single thing ; a paragraph, a single thing ; an essay, a single thing. Each part is to be a preliminary whole, and the total a finished whole. But the ability to construct one thing out of many does not come by nature. It implies fecundity, restraint, an eye for effects, the forecast of finish while we are still working in the rough, obedience to the demands of development, and a deaf ear to whatever calls us into the by-paths of caprice ; in short, it implies that the good writer is to be an artist.

Now something of this large requirement which composition makes, the young writer instinctively feels, and he is terrified. He knows how ill-fitted he is to direct "toil coöperant to an end ; " and when he sits down to the desk and sees the white sheet of paper before him, he shivers.

IN ENGLISH

Let him know that the shiver is a suitable part of the performance. I well remember the pleasure with which, as a young man, I heard my venerable and practised professor of rhetoric say that he supposed there was no work known to man more difficult than writing. Up to that time I had supposed its severities peculiar to myself. It cheered me, and gave me courage to try again, to learn that I had all mankind for my fellow-sufferers. Where this is not understood, writing is avoided. From such avoidance I would save the young writer by my precept to seek every opportunity to write. For most of us this is a new way of confronting composition — treating it as an opportunity, a chance, and not as a burden or compulsion. It saves from slavishness and takes away the drudgery of writing, to view each piece of it as a precious and necessary step in the pathway to power. To those engaged in bread-winning employments these opportunities will be few. Spring forward to them, then, using them to the full. Severe they will be because so few, for only practice breeds ease; but on that very account let no one of them pass with merely a

27

second-best performance. If a letter is to be written to a friend, a report to an employer, a communication to a newspaper, see that it has a beginning, a middle, and an end. The majority of writings are without these pleasing adornments. Only the great pieces possess them. Bear this in mind, and win the way to artistic composition by noticing what should be said first, what second, and what third.

I cannot leave this subject, however, without congratulating the present generation on its advantages over mine. Children are brought up to-day, in happy contrast with my compeers, to feel that the pencil is no instrument of torture, hardly indeed to distinguish it from the tongue. About the time they leave their mother's arms they take their pen in hand. On paper they are encouraged to describe their interesting birds, friends, adventures. Their written lessons are almost as frequent as their oral, and they learn to write compositions while not yet quite understanding what they are about. Some of these fortunate ones will, I hope, find the language I have sadly used about the difficulty of writing extravagant. And let me say, too, that since frequency has more to do with ease of writing than anything else, I count the newspaper men lucky because they are writing all the time, and I do not think so meanly of their product as the present popular disparagement would seem to require. It is hasty work undoubtedly, and bears the marks of haste. But in my judgment, at no period of the English language has there been so high an average of sensible, vivacious, and informing sentences written as appears in our daily press. With both good and evil results, the distinction between book literature and speech literature is breaking down. Everybody is writing, apparently in verse and prose ; and if the higher graces of style do not often appear, neither on the other hand do the ruder awkwardnesses and obscurities. A certain straightforward English is becoming established. A whole nation is learning the use of its mother-tongue. Under such circumstances it is doubly necessary that any one who is conscious of feebleness in his command of English should promptly and earnestly begin the cultivation of it.

SELF-CULTIVATION

My third precept shall be, "Remember the other person." I have been urging self-cultivation in English as if it concerned one person alone, ourself. But every utterance really concerns two. Its aim is social. Its object is communication; and while unquestionably prompted half-way by the desire to ease our mind through self-expression, it still finds its only justification in the advantage somebody else will draw from what is said. Speaking or writing is, therefore, everywhere a double-ended process. It springs from me, it penetrates him; and both of these ends need watching. Is what I say precisely what I mean? That is an important question. Is what I say so shaped that it can readily be assimilated by him who hears? This is a question of quite as great consequence, and much more likely to be forgotten. We are so full of ourselves that we do not remember the other person. Helter-skelter we pour forth our unaimed words merely for our personal relief, heedless whether they help or hinder him whom they still purport to address. For most of us are grievously lacking in imagination, which is the ability to go outside ourselves and take on the conditions of another mind. Yet this is what the literary artist is always doing. He has at once the ability to see for himself and the ability to see himself as others see him. He can lead two lives as easily as one life ; or rather, he has trained himself to consider that other life as of more importance than his, and to reckon his comfort, likings, and labors as quite subordinated to the service of that other. All serious literary work contains within it this readiness to bear another's burden. I must write with pains, that he may read with ease. I must

> Find out men's wants and wills,
> And meet them *there*.

As I write, I must unceasingly study what is the line of least intellectual resistance along which my thought may enter the differently constituted mind ; and to that line I must subtly adjust, without enfeebling, my meaning. Will this combination of words or that make the meaning clear ? Will this order of presentation facilitate swiftness of apprehension, or will it clog the movement ? What temperamental perversities in me must be set aside in order to render my reader's approach to what I would tell him pleasant? What temperamental perversities in him must be accepted by me as fixed facts, conditioning all I say? These are the questions the skillful writer is always asking.

And these questions, as will have been perceived already, are moral questions no less than literary. That golden rule of generous service by which we do for others what we would have them do for us, is a rule of writing too. Every writer who knows his trade perceives that he is a servant, that it is his business to endure hardship if only his reader may win freedom from toil, that no impediment to that reader's understanding is too slight to deserve diligent attention, that he has consequently no right to let a single sentence slip from him unsocialized — I mean, a sentence which cannot become as naturally another's possession as his own. In the very act of asserting himself, he lays aside what is distinctively his. And because these qualifications of the writer are moral qualifications, they can never be completely fulfilled so long as we live and write. We may continually approximate them more nearly, but there will still always be possible an alluring refinement of exercise beyond. The world of the literary artist and the moral man is interesting through its inexhaustibility : and he who serves his fellows by writing or by speech is artist and moral man in one. Writing a letter is a simple matter, but it is a moral matter and an artistic; for it may be done either with imagination or with raw self-centredness. What things will my correspondent wish to know ? How can I transport him out of his properly alien surroundings into the vivid impressions which now are mine ? How can I tell all I long to tell and still be sure the telling will be for him as lucid and delightful as for me ? Remember the other person, I say. Do not become absorbed in yourself. Your interests cover only the half of any piece of writing; the other man's less visible half is necessary to complete yours. And if I have here discussed writing more than speech, that is merely because when we speak we utter our first thoughts, but when we write, our second, — or better still, our fourth ; and in the greater deliberation which writing affords I have felt that the demands of morality and art, which are universally imbedded in language, could be more distinctly perceived. Yet none the less truly do we need to talk for the other person than to write for him.

But there remains a fourth weighty precept, and one not altogether detachable from the third. It is this: "Lean upon your subject." We have seen how the user of language, whether in writing or in speaking, works for himself; how he works for another individual too; but there is one more for whom his work is performed, one of greater consequence than any person, and that is his subject. From this comes his primary call. Those who in their utterance fix their thoughts on themselves, or on other selves, never reach power. That resides in the subject. There we must dwell with it, and be content to have no other strength than its. When the frightened school-boy sits down to write about Spring, he cannot imagine where the thoughts which are to make up his piece are to come from. He cudgels his brain for ideas. He examines his pen-point, the curtains, his inkstand, to see if perhaps ideas may not be had from these. He wonders what his teacher will wish him to say, and he tries to recall how the passage sounded in the Third Reader. In every direction but one he turns, and that is the direction where lies the prime mover of his toil, his subject. Of that he is afraid. Now, what I want to make evident is that this subject is not in reality the foe, but the friend. It is his only helper. His composition is not to be, as he seems to suppose, a mass of his laborious inventions, but it is to be made up exclusively of what the subject dictates. He has only to attend. At present he stands in his own way, making such a din with his private anxieties that he cannot hear the rich suggestions of the subject. He is bothered with considering how he feels, or what he or somebody else will like to see on his paper. This is debilitating business. He must lean on his subject, if he would have his writing strong, and busy himself with what it says, rather than with what he would say. Matthew Arnold, in the important preface to his poems of 1853, contrasting the artistic methods of Greek poetry and modern poetry, sums up the teaching of the Greeks in these words : " All depends upon the subject ; choose a fitting action, penetrate yourself with the feeling of its situations ; this done, everything else will follow." And he calls attention to the self-assertive and scatter-brained habits of our time. " How different a way of thinking from this is ours ! We can hardly at the present day understand what Menander meant, when he told a man who inquired as to the progress of his comedy that he had finished it, not having yet written a single line, because he had constructed the action of it in his mind. A modern critic would have assured him that the merit of his piece depended on the brilliant things which arose under his pen as he went along. I verily think that the majority of us do not in our hearts believe that there is such a thing as a total impression to be derived from a poem, or to be demanded from a poet. We permit the poet to select any action he pleases, and to suffer that action to go as it will, provided he gratifies us with occasional bursts of fine writing, and with a shower of isolated thoughts and images."

IN ENGLISH

Great writers put themselves and their personal imaginings out of sight. Their writing becomes a kind of transparent window on which reality is reflected, and through which people see, not them, but that of which they write. How much we know of Shakespeare's characters! How little of Shakespeare! Of him that might almost be said which Isaiah said of God, " He hideth himself." The best writer is the best mental listener, the one who peers farthest into his matter and most fully heeds its behests. Preëminently obedient is the strong writer, — refinedly, energetically obedient. I once spent a day with a great novelist when the book which subsequently proved his masterpiece was only half written. I praised his mighty hero, but said I should think the life of an author would be miserable who, having created a character so huge, now had him in hand and must find something for him to do. My friend seemed puzzled by my remark, but after a moment's pause said, " I don't think you know how we work. I have nothing to do with the character. Now that he is created, he will act as he will."

And such docility must be cultivated by every

one who would write well, such strenuous docility. Of course there must be energy in plenty;
the imagination which I described in my third
section, the passion for solid form as in my
second, the disciplined and daring powers as in
my first; but all these must be ready at a
moment's notice to move where the matter calls
and to acknowledge that all their worth is to be
drawn from it. Religion is only enlarged good
sense, and the words of Jesus apply as well to
the things of earth as of heaven. I do not know
where we could find a more compendious state-
ment of what is most important for one to learn
who would cultivate himself in English than the
simple saying in which Jesus announces the
source of his power. "The word which ye hear
is not mine, but the Father's which sent me."
Whoever can use such words will be a noble
speaker indeed.

These, then, are the fundamental precepts
which every one must heed who would command
our beautiful English language. There is, of
course, a fifth. I hardly need to name it; for it
always follows after, whatever others precede.

IN ENGLISH

It is that we should do the work, and not think about it ; do it day after day and not grow weary in bad doing. Early and often we must be busy, and be satisfied to have a great deal of labor produce but a small result. I am told that early in life John Morley, wishing to engage in journalism, wrote an editorial and sent it to a paper every day for nearly a year before he succeeded in getting one accepted. We all know what a power he became in London journalism. I will not vouch for the truth of this story, but I am sure an ambitious author is wise who writes a weekly essay for his stove. Publication is of little consequence, so long as one is getting one's self hammered into shape.

But before I close this address, let me acknowledge that in it I have neglected a whole class of helpful influences, probably quite as important as any I have discussed. Purposely I have passed them by. Because I wished to show what we can do for ourselves, I have everywhere assumed that our cultivation in English is to be effected by naked volition and a kind of dead lift. These are mighty agencies, but seldom in this interlocked world do they work well alone. They are strongest when backed by social suggestion and unconscious custom. Ordinarily the good speaker is he who keeps good company, but increases the helpful influence of that company by constant watchfulness along the lines I have marked out. So supplemented, my teaching is true. By itself it is not true. It needs the supplementation of others. Let him who would speak or write well seek out good speakers and writers. Let him live in their society, — for the society of the greatest writers is open to the most secluded, — let him feel the ease of their excellence, the ingenuity, grace, and scope of their diction, and he will soon find in himself capacities whose development may be aided by the precepts I have given. Most of us catch better than we learn. We take up unconsciously from our surroundings what we cannot altogether create. All this should be remembered, and we should keep ourselves exposed to the wholesome words of our fellow-men. Yet our own exertions will not on that account be rendered less important. We may largely choose the influences to which we submit ; we may exercise a selective attention among these influences ; we may enjoy, oppose, modify, or diligently ingraft what is conveyed to us, — and for doing any one of these things rationally we must be guided by some clear aim. Such aims, altogether essential even if subsidiary, I have sought to supply ; and I would reiterate that he who holds them fast may become superior to linguistic fortune and be the wise director of his sluggish and obstinate tongue. It is as certain as anything can be that faithful endeavor will bring expertness in the use of English. If we are watchful of our speech, making our words continually more minutely true, free, and resourceful ; if we look upon our occasions of writing as opportunities for the deliberate work of unified construction; if in all our utterances we think of him who hears as well as of him who speaks ; and above all, if we fix the attention of ourselves and our hearers on the matter we talk about and so let ourselves be supported by our subject, — we shall make a daily advance not only in English study, but in personal power, in general serviceableness, and in consequent delight.

OUTLINE

THE MASTERY OF ENGLISH AS A TOOL

LOOK WELL TO YOUR SPEECH

WELCOME EVERY OPPORTUNITY FOR WRITING

REMEMBER THE OTHER PERSON

LEAN UPON YOUR SUBJECT

WORK DAY AFTER DAY UNWEARYINGLY

SEEK THE COMPANY OF GOOD SPEAKERS AND WRITERS

The Riverside Press

CAMBRIDGE . MASSACHUSETTS

U . S . A

Riverside Educational Monographs

Editor, HENRY SUZZALLO, Professor of The Philosophy of Education, Teachers College, Columbia University, New York.

NUMBERS READY OR IN PREPARATION

General Educational Theory

EDUCATION. An essay and other selections. By RALPH WALDO EMERSON. *Ready.*

THE MEANING OF INFANCY, and The Part Played by Infancy in the Evolution of Man. By JOHN FISKE. *Ready.*

EDUCATION FOR EFFICIENCY, and The New Definition of the Cultivated Man. By CHARLES W. ELIOT, President of Harvard University. *Ready.*

MORAL PRINCIPLES IN EDUCATION. By JOHN DEWEY, Professor of Philosophy, Columbia University. *Ready.*

OUR NATIONAL IDEALS IN EDUCATION. By ELMER E. BROWN, United States Commissioner of Education. *In preparation.*

THE SCHOOL AS A SOCIAL INSTITUTION. By HENRY SUZZALLO, Professor of the Philosophy of Education, Teachers College, Columbia University. *In preparation.*

Administration and Supervision of Schools

CONTINUATION SCHOOLS. By PAUL H. HANUS, Professor of Education, Harvard University. *In preparation.*

CHANGING CONCEPTIONS OF EDUCATION. By E. P. CUBBERLY, Professor of Education, Leland Stanford Jr. University. *In preparation.*

THE SUPERVISION OF SCHOOLS. By Henry Suzzallo, Professor of the Philosophy of Education, Teachers College, Columbia University. *In preparation.*

Methods of Teaching

SELF-CULTIVATION IN ENGLISH. By GEORGE HERBERT PALMER, Professor of Philosophy, Harvard University. *Ready.*

ETHICAL AND MORAL INSTRUCTION IN SCHOOLS. By GEORGE HERBERT PALMER, Professor of Philosophy, Harvard University. *Ready.*

TEACHING CHILDREN TO STUDY. By LIDA B. EARHART, Instructor in Elementary Education, Teachers College, Columba University. (*Double Number.*) *Ready.*

TYPES OF TEACHING. By FREDERIC ERNEST FARRINGTON, Associate Professor of Education, University of Texas. *In preparation.*

Price 35 cents, each, net, postpaid

HOUGHTON MIFFLIN COMPANY

BOSTON   NEW YORK   CHICAGO